# COLLECT TH[E]

**Boffin Boy and the Rock Men**
by David Orme

Illustrated by Peter Richardson

Published by Ransom Publishing Ltd.
51 Southgate Street, Winchester, Hants. SO23 9EH
www.ransom.co.uk

ISBN   978 184167 624 1
First published in 2007
Reprinted 2008, 2009
Copyright © 2007 Ransom Publishing Ltd.

Illustrations copyright © 2007 Peter Richardson

A CIP catalogue record of this book is available from the British Library.

Design & layout: *www.macwiz.co.uk*

Find out more about Boffin Boy at *www.ransom.co.uk*.

# Boffin Boy
## AND THE
## Rock Men

By David Orme
Illustrated by Peter Richardson

Ransom

I'm your Rock Man and the perfect pet!
No need to feed me!
No need to take me for walks!
If you get tired of me, just plug me
into your computer, and I'll turn
into someone else!
Carefully made just for you by
LUBRA TOYS, Zone City.

Before long, people got fed up with their Rock Men. But they didn't have to go and buy a new one. They could plug them into their computer and turn them into different Rock Men . . .

# ABOUT THE AUTHOR

David Orme has written over 200 books including poetry collections, fiction and non-fiction, and school text books. When he is not writing books he travels around the UK, giving performances, running writing workshops and courses.

Find out more at:
*www.magic-nation.com.*